How to Ruin Your Love Life

Other Hay House Titles by Ben Stein

How to Ruin Your Life
(also available as an audiocassette and CD)

How to Ruin Your Financial Life
(available April 2004)

♡♡♡♡

Hay House Titles of Related Interest

Books

Feng Shui Dos & Taboos for Love, by Angi Ma Wong

Getting Unstuck: *8 Simple Steps to Solving Any Problem,*
by Dr. Joy Browne

**The Relationship Problem Solver for Love,
Marriage, and Dating,** by Kelly E. Johnson, M.D.

Secrets of Attraction:
The Universal Laws of Love, Sex, and Romance,
by Sandra Anne Taylor

Card Decks

Manifesting Good Luck Cards:
Love and Relationships, by Deepak Chopra

Heart and Soul, by Sylvia Browne

I Can Do It® Cards:
Affirmations for Romance, by Louise L. Hay

MarsVenus Cards, by John Gray

All of the above are available at your local bookstore,
or may be ordered through Hay House, Inc.:

(800) 654-5126 or **(760) 431-7695**
(800) 650-5115 (fax) or **(760) 431-6948 (fax)**

www.hayhouse.com (Hay House USA)
www.hayhouse.com.au (Hay House Australia)
www.hayhouse.co.uk (Hay House U.K.)

How to Ruin Your Love Life

Ben Stein

HAY HOUSE, INC.
Carlsbad, California
London • Sydney • Johannesburg
Vancouver • Hong Kong

Published and distributed in the United States by: Hay House, Inc.,
P.O. Box 5100, Carlsbad, CA 92018-5100 • *Phone:* (760) 431-7695 or
(800) 654-5126 • *Fax:* (760) 431-6948 or (800) 650-5115 •
www.hayhouse.com • **Published and distributed in Australia by:**
Hay House Australia Ltd., 18/36 Ralph St., Alexandria NSW 2015 •
Phone: 612-9669-4299 • *Fax:* 612-9669-4144 • www.hayhouse.com.au •
Published and distributed in the United Kingdom by:
Hay House UK, Ltd. • Unit 202, Canalot Studios • 222 Kensal Rd.,
London W10 5BN • *Phone:* 44-20-8962-1230 • *Fax:* 44-20-8962-1239 •
www.hayhouse.co.uk • **Published and distributed in the Republic
of South Africa by:** Hay House SA (Pty), Ltd., P.O. Box 990, Witkoppen
2068 • *Phone/Fax:* 2711-7012233 • orders@psdprom.co.za • **Distributed
in Canada by:** Raincoast • 9050 Shaughnessy St., Vancouver, B.C. V6P
6E5 • *Phone:* (604) 323-7100 • *Fax:* (604) 323-2600

Editorial supervision: Jill Kramer   *Design:* Tricia Breidenthal

Library of Congress Cataloging-in-Publication Data

Stein, Ben.
  How to ruin your love life / Ben Stein.
      p. cm.
  ISBN 1-4019-0240-5 (cloth) — ISBN 1-4019-0285-5 (cloth gift edition)
  1. Man-woman relationships—Humor. 2. Love—Humor. 3. Conduct of
life—Humor. I. Title.
  HQ801.S795 2003
  306.7—dc21

                              2003009784

                         ISBN 1-4019-0240-5
                  Special Edition ISBN: 1-4019-0285-5

                    06 05 04 03   5 4 3 2
                      1st printing, August 2003
                     2nd printing, September 2003

                Printed in the United States of America

CONTENTS

♡♡♡♡

How to Ruin Your Love Life:

♡♡♡♡

*For Alex, my saintly wife,
and for all good dogs and cats.*

♡♡♡♡

ACKNOWLEDGMENTS

♡♡♡♡

Thank you to all of the fine people at Hay House for your help with this book, particularly:

Louise L. Hay, founder/chairman and endless inspiration; Reid Tracy, president/CEO, who believed in this concept from day one; Jill Kramer, editorial director and tireless colleague; Tonya Toone, cheery and resourceful publicist; Christy Salinas, talented creative director; Amy Rose Szalkiewicz and Tricia Breidenthal, fine graphic designers; Danny Levin, business development, who also "got it" about these books right away; and Monique Mallory, fabulous freelance publicist out of New York.

I'd also like to thank my agent, Lois Wallace, with whom I have had the longest professional association I've ever had with anyone in my life.

INTRODUCTION

♡♡♡♡

"Man is born free, but everywhere is in chains." So said the great philosopher Rousseau more than 200 years ago. He was referring to a political situation in which almost all of the people in the world lived under monarchic despots.

My experience of life compels me to make a similar observation, or series of observations. Man and woman would be happiest in a lasting, loving relationship, but everywhere they're alone and miserable.

Or, perhaps I can break this down into a series of premises.

Premise #1: Being in a lasting, loving, sharing, caring relationship would seem to be a superb way to live life, as the poets and novelists and psychiatrists all agree. Being in love and being able to share love with someone else is one of the keystones of the structure of a fulfilled life—perhaps it's the *definitive* foundation of a fulfilled life. The only possible competitor for such a basic building block of life would be being happy in one's work, and love is usually considered even more important than that. It really is impossible to be happy and alone on a long-term basis.

Premise #2: A lot of people are unhappy, alone, and loveless, despite a world that offers a cornucopia of opportunities for love. A vast and unhappy army of men and women marches in solitary lockstep through daily life, wondering why they're unhappy . . . and yet they remain alone.

Premise #3: In this life, we generally make our own experience. What happens to us in a free society is, within large limits, almost completely made up of what we do to ourselves. Or, as a fan of my previous book *How to Ruin Your Life* told me in an e-mail: "I have begun to realize that I have some part in what happens to me." *Some part* indeed. Except for cases of accidental death or injury, or chronic and/or disabling illness, men and women in a free, prosperous society like ours generally create their own reality.

This reality can be filled with love and caring, or it can be filled with . . . well, emptiness, anger, and frustration. It's largely up to the individual man or woman to make that reality incredibly good or preposterously bad. And please don't say that your reality is shaped by beauty or lack of beauty resulting from birth or height or accent or place of origin. The most cursory nod at engagement columns and at couples at Disneyland tells us that there's a lid for every pot if only the lid and the pot will consent to make themselves fit together. The same is true about wealth and poverty, education and lack thereof. Persons from every background can find love—or they can find loneliness. It's very largely up to the individual.

This book is a humorous way for you, the reader, to realize how to make yourself fit into loving relationships, by telling you how *not* to fit into a lonely, rage-filled life. It is, if you will, a road map in reverse, as I said about my first *How to Ruin* book, with sure guides to getting where you want to go—by simply *not* going where you *do not* want to go.

How did I come to write this book? In my life, I am cursed—as my mother, father, and sister were and are—by a habit of categorization. I see some examples, make a hypothesis based upon them, test that hypothesis, and if it works, I adopt it as a predictor and explainer of the human condition. For example, many decades ago, my sister ventured the following brilliant hypo about mankind: "Your basic human," she said, "is not such a hot item."

How true that has turned out to be.

I especially look for examples, observations, generalizations, and then rules about love, since love is the ruling passion in my life. And I particularly try to determine why so many men and women I know go without love in their lives on an ongoing basis. In my own little circle here in glorious Los Angeles, I have women friends who are stunningly beautiful yet who are alone and miserable most of the time. I've watched them carefully to see what they do each day in their social and love relationships (such as they are), and what specifically they do that keeps them alone. I've been blessed in knowing some women who are so spectacularly good at warding off love that they've inspired me to want to write down what they're doing. (In fact, just observing what some of these women are up to and writing it down has provided me with much of the material for this book.)

I've also seen many men—handsome, well-off, sharply dressed men—who are pitifully alone. I was moved to sit down at my word processor by the catalog of what they're doing wrong in their love relationships. They, too, helped me write much of this book.

As I gathered material on these lost souls, I realized that they had given me not just random axioms, but a thorough, complete, and effective set of rules on how to ruin a love relationship—or how to never have one at all. And even better, they'd given me a set of rules on how to have a decent love relationship—if only one followed these steps in reverse. That is, if you can learn the rules of how to ruin your love life and then do the opposite, you are on your way to having a good, lasting love relationship.

Easier said than done, since people operate largely out of compulsion, but then here comes a key part: You must, if you wish to have any success at love, take responsibility for your own life and for what happens to you . . . and then overcome these compulsions. If you're going to say that you act out of deep-seated compulsion and you'll never get any better—and if you truly believe that—you really *will* get to spend your whole life alone and miserable. If you realize that successful men and women can and do overcome their compulsions little by little, you can and will triumph.

I've tried to make it easy for you in this book—at least I hope I have. Since these rules tend to be humorous, perhaps they'll go down easier than if they were laid down as some sort of Prussian marching manual—humorless, strict, and unforgiving. That was, at least, my thought. Follow these rules and you have loneliness. Do the opposite, and you have love in your life. It's that simple.

I want to note that I also had some other sources of inspiration, though, besides the people who did it all wrong. Specifically, I had some ideas on how to do it all right.

By pure luck and God's grace, I'm married to a woman of almost preternatural saintliness and lovability, if that is a word. She makes absolutely none of the mistakes that I lay out here as ways to ruin your love life. I must confess that some of these rules are derived simply by noting what my wife does and recommending that you do the opposite in order to ruin your love life. That is, my wife has been so amazingly good at preserving her love life with her difficult husband that I can fairly recommend that you do the opposite of what she does if you want to *wreck* your love life. I tested this plan or approach and found that it worked well. The people who were alone really did do the opposite of what my wife does, and so the rules work out from that origin as well. My wife's name is Alexandra Denman, and I thank her profusely.

Also, I have some friends who are brilliant at understanding the dynamics of relationships. They've supplied me with examples of how to wreck love lives based on their own experience and observations. I specifically thank super-smart Philip DeMuth, Ph.D., in psychology; dear friend Paul Hyman, M.D., psychoanalyst and genius; Al Burton, best friend and shrewd observer; Tetyana Terasova-Abel, medical student; and Mike Long, brilliant young writer. Their contributions were invaluable.

I'm sure that I've missed some vital rules here, and for that I apologize. But as you read these rules, please remember that beginning and ending each and every one of them are two Super Rules for ruining your love life, which should be integrated into every other rule here. In fact, if you just follow these two rules, I assure you that you'll be far down the road to loneliness and despair:

One:
YOU ARE BETTER THAN ANYONE ELSE.
And two:
NEVER FORGIVE AND NEVER FORGET.

With that, happy reading, and happy trails.

How to
Ruin Your
Love
Life

1

♡♡♡♡

Know That Your Wishes Are the Only Ones That Matter in Any Situation

Something that you're going to have to get into your little pumpkin head is that your lover basically exists to help you. He has no meaningful life independent of what he can do for you. Yes, your lover may have what some might see as personal interests, hobbies, needs, wishes, and fears, but those aren't important. What *is* important, what *does* count, is what your lover can *do for you*. If he's interested in playing tennis or buying antiques or watching the Tampa Bay Buccaneers on TV, that's worthy of some tiny, passing notice. And if he has some desire to live a life that has some modicum of independence to it, that's also interesting, ho-hum. You might acknowledge it with a cursory nod and a wave.

But what really counts in any relationship is *you!* What *you* want from the relationship is what matters. What *you* want out of your lover is what always comes first in any and every situation.

If your lover wants to stay home and listen to opera—or even sing along with Ludacris on the stereo—that's nice, and you might say how cute he is for having that desire. But what really matters is what *you* want to do. If you decide that you simply have to go shopping for furniture on this particular day, then that's what you're both going to do. If you have to go to the mall and want to drag your lover along, no matter how unhappy he looks, then that's the deciding vote. (By the way, you *always* cast the deciding vote about everything.) If you want to go to a friend's house and watch old movies and drink cocktails on a Saturday night while your lover sits home alone, then that's the way it has to be.

If you feel that you don't want to go on a vacation and your lover does, then just stay home and watch him stew in his own juices. You see, your goal here is to express in words and actions that *your* wishes are the only ones that matter.

The truth is that your "love object" is incredibly, unbelievably lucky to have you in his life. Just for this unworthy soul to be associated with you is such a grand honor that you don't really need to pay any further attention to his desires.

Plus, the truth is, and this is so important that it deserves its own rule . . .

2

♡ ♡ ♡ ♡

Rest Assured That You Know Better about Every Subject Than Your Lover

This is not particularly a matter of education or who went to what college or graduate school. This is not about your thinking that you know better because you have a Ph.D. in psychology and your lover is a high-school dropout. No, this has to do with the fact that you, just for being *you,* know better than your lover about everything. You know better about sports, food, and clothing. You know better about her family. You especially know better about her friends.

You just plain know better about everything. You can save a lot of future aggravation and pain if you just make that clear early on. Yes, you may listen briefly to your lover's opinions (never facts—always, at best, opinions) and nod politely and pityingly at them. But are they truly deserving of being heard? Is it really worth the time of someone as smart as you to hear such low-order blathering? I don't think so, and neither do you.

You know better about who to hang out with, who to be around, who not to be around, where to live, what to buy, and what not to buy.

And you know what? Get that idea out in the open right away. Don't waste a moment with any kind of fake solicitude for your lover's nattering. Just express here and now that you're the smart one in the relationship and things will go better for both of you.

You see, the sad truth is that if your lover gets the idea into her head that her ideas are worth anything, then she's going to be as disappointed as can be when you finally have to bring the hammer down and let her know that, in fact, her ideas are, well, not quite "worthless," but not really up to your level or anything close to it. If you can get her acclimated right away to the crucial truth that she really has very little of worth to say on anything important, then you're far ahead of the game in terms of time-saving and getting lines of authority set down neatly.

And please don't be worried about hurting her feelings because, if I may make so obvious a point, you can . . .

3

♡♡♡♡

Live Your Life As If Only <u>Your</u> Feelings Count!

Now, I don't for a moment mean to say that your lover doesn't have any feelings. That would be totally incorrect and an insult to the whole idea of humanity. All human beings have feelings. In fact, the key to what distinguishes human beings from rocks and stones is that humans have feelings. Your lover *does* have feelings of joy, exhilaration, fear, loss, torment, and despair. Have no doubt about that. The only thing is that those feelings don't really count for much in the grand scheme of things. Oh, sure, to him, those feelings may seem important at the moment, but overall, in the big picture, your lover's feelings just don't mean very much. After all, *you* are not feeling them!

7

No, *you* are feeling *your* feelings, and those are the ones that matter. In fact, each feeling you have counts for about 1,000 times as much as each feeling that your lover has. Again, this is simply because *you* can feel *your* own feelings and you cannot—if you are in the mood to ruin your love life at all—feel his.

Now, those are some of the Grand Rules of Disengagement, the overarching principles that govern how your relationship with your lover will be run so that it cannot possibly last. But there are dozens of smaller rules governing specific situations, and you need to hear about these to really wreck your love life.

Let's try a few of them. . . .

4

♡ ♡ ♡ ♡

Point Out Your Lover's Imperfections in Public

You've probably been very restrained about pointing out your lover's failings up till now. You've no doubt observed them, catalogued them, and made them into neat lists in your head. But most likely, out of some excess of politeness, you've refrained from revealing each one to her. Maybe you didn't want to start an argument when other people weren't around, because what would be the point? You want *others* to notice how totally right you are, too. An audience of one just doesn't cut it. After all, what's the point of noting that your girlfriend never dresses in coordinated clothes and has a blubber roll if there's no one there to cheer you on and laugh appreciatively at your verbal repartee and biting wit? Entertainers act in front of cheering throngs, not in closets.

That's why it's urgent that you save up all of your gripes and unload them all at once on your lover when other people are nearby. For example, suppose you think that your girlfriend is a little too close to her mother and talks to her on the phone far too much. Fine. The best time to make that observation is not when the two of you are alone together. No, how can you get a laugh out of a grown woman you've just accused of being a big baby? You can't. Wait until you have friends over for dinner. Wait until you're at a cocktail party slurping down Grey Goose. Then, when everyone's a bit tipsy and in a mood to laugh, say, "Oh, Cindy wouldn't even dream of going through a day without talking to her mother. She wrote the book on being Mother's perfect little girl. Not that I mind, but she *is* 38, so you might think she could go through a day without asking her mommy what to wear every day."

That way, you get a few laughs. Plus, you brand your lover as a weak, immature, ineffectual female whose friends all now know it to be true. How *clever* you are!

Now she's probably going to be a little ticked off at you when you get home that night. After all, you've just humiliated her in front of her friends. She might even berate you for it.

Well, that's when you get to lay in your next
ultra-cool step to ruining your love life
and make it happen in living color. . . .

5

♡♡♡♡

Never Admit That You're Wrong or Apologize in Any Dispute

Why should you ever admit that you're wrong? You are *never* wrong. Just the fact that *you* did it or said it or forgot to do it makes it right. That, by itself, converts wrong to right. Maybe you recall your high school teachers teaching you about "the divine right of kings," which basically meant that they were appointed by God and could do no wrong. Well, that was long abolished by revolutions, and heads rolled that were supposedly divinely blessed. But *you* still have that divine right, and it means that you're never, ever wrong.

Now, let's imagine that your boyfriend starts in on you by accusing you of humiliating him in front of his friends at a public gathering. Well, just laugh at him some more, and tell him he's a wimp for not being able to take a joke. Or tell him that when you called him a mama's boy in front of his college buddies and he didn't get a kick out of it, well, that just proves how weak and overly sensitive he is.

Or, let's say the shoe's on the other foot. Suppose you're the guy and you've just said—in front of your friends—that your girlfriend or wife is a total slob who can't even keep her shoe rack straight, let alone balance a checkbook. And it just so happens that she works as a bookkeeper at a shoe store, so the criticism, leveled in front of her colleagues from The Shoe Giant really stings. And she tells you so. What do you do? Well, you simply say, "Hey, if the shoe fits, wear it." Or else, just look at her sternly and say, "I guess you just can't take the truth, right? I'm just trying to help, but if you can't accept the fact that you're a slob, then I guess that just shows how insecure you are. Maybe that's the source of your slobbiness."

(By the way, human beings love to be told how insecure they are. It makes them feel swell. Try it over and over again—you'll be amazed by how it makes people love you.)

Or else just say, "Hey, I call 'em like I see 'em, and if you can't take it, tough."

The main idea is that you should absolutely refuse to apologize for being wrong . . . because you never are. The burden is always on your lover to simply take your criticism and bear it.

And if you won't admit that her feelings have any merit, that's just fine. Your lover should get used to the idea that what she has to say means zilch, nothing, and that any expectation that you'll pay real attention to what she says is a joke.

Just forget apologies no matter what you do, and this doesn't just apply to what you say. Suppose you come home drunk and knock over your wife's favorite vase and smash it. Don't apologize. If you crash into your husband's car in the garage, for goodness' sake, don't say you're sorry.

If your wife catches you flirting with her co-worker, don't apologize. You owe it to yourself to never admit you're wrong. It might give you some kind of complex if you start doing so. Just don't do it, period. If you said it or did it, or didn't say it or didn't do it, that makes it right.

6

♡ ♡ ♡ ♡

Overdramatize Everything

Turn everything that happens to you into high drama. Don't let anything just be a normal part of someone's day. No, you have to have excitement and turbulence in your life. If your lover does the slightest thing you don't like, make it into a huge scene filled with anguish and recrimination. If she does anything that's even slightly wrong around the house, make it into an aggravated crime. There's nothing that you can't make into the mad scene of Ophelia in *Hamlet* if you really try. Make your mate really suffer and sweat bullets over any little thing that goes amiss in your life. It's not just an incident—it's the stuff of horror movies, and don't you forget it.

Be sure to save up all of your energy for these scenes. If your lover overfills a cup of tea, scream as if she's just pulled a gun on you. If she asks you about something you charged on your joint credit card, have a fit and scream at the top of your lungs that what you do is none of her business. If she asks if you want to see a movie, act as if she's insulted you by suggesting that you go see that piece of cinematic trash.

It's also important to make a huge deal about everything that happened to you during the day when you come home from work. Turn every event into the shower scene from *Psycho* so that it's really unpleasant and tense for your lover to have a conversation with you. This makes total sense. It allows you to occupy the stage and to give yourself the lead role in whatever drama you've decided to play out that day. You don't need to audition or go to acting school. You can have your drama anytime you want—and if it's too much for your lover to bear on a constant basis, too bad. If you want to go into hysterics recalling the conversation you had with your boss that day, go for it.

You have the right to create unpleasant, irrational dramas in your life any and all of the time. That is your right as a diva, male or female.

7

♡♡♡♡

Demand Expensive Gifts from Your Lover

That's right. Just having your boyfriend love you, praise you, or pay attention to you isn't enough. You want something tangible that you can actually put in your jewelry box or on your stereo shelf. Don't let him get away with just saying or doing sweet things. No, you want the equivalent of gold doubloons that the pirate captain would bite on to make sure it was real gold. You want something that you can show off to your friends—and how can you wear a sweet phrase around your neck?

There's a great song about diamonds being a girl's best friend—and you know what? It's totally true. Diamonds *are* a girl's best friend. But gold rings and fancy cars and pearl necklaces are nice, too.

Now suppose your boyfriend can't afford to give you lavish presents. Well, then mock and belittle him—preferably in front of other people. Now you're getting it. Nothing should inhibit you from letting fly with some really caustic comments if you're not getting the goods. How's this for a good one: "My last boyfriend always gave me gold jewelry, but Tom here has never even taken me out to a five-star restaurant for dinner!"

In today's world, talk is cheap. But money walks the walk *and* talks the talk. That's why you need some concrete evidence of how much your lover cares for you in the form of something with a fancy price tag. Only if you can gaze at something really extravagant on your wrist or in your study can you be sure that you're getting all you truly deserve.

8

♡ ♡ ♡ ♡

Never Be Grateful for the Gifts You <u>Do</u> Get

True, they may have been a major drain on his salary. Yes, they may have required her to work overtime to pay for the gifts. But if you act really grateful, that implies some sense of duty or obligation on your part. Bad idea! Just accept the gifts you receive, give correct but not effusive thanks, and let it be known that you expect even better next time.

That way, you let your lover know that he's never quite adequate, never quite getting all the way there in terms of making you happy—and that he has to try harder next time.

Now, some may say, "Hey, isn't love about *sharing?* Isn't it about taking up burdens and bearing them jointly? It's not about just one of you exploiting the other, is it?"

Well, I'm so glad you brought that up.
Because the truth is . . .

9

♡ ♡ ♡ ♡

Carve It in Stone: Love Relationships Aren't Partnerships— They're Master-Servant Relationships, and You Are the Master (or Mistress)

What kind of fun is it if you have to share things? How is it fair to be expected to do as much for the other person as he does for you? I mean, how do you come out ahead in that situation?

No, you're owed everything you can get from the relationship, and in return, you're supposed to give as little as humanly possible and still generate enough interest to get the gifts and the attention and adoration. Imagine the relationship between a master and a slave in the old South—and there you have your template of the kind of relationship you should have. You get the adoration, and he gets the opportunity to adore. You get the gifts, and he gets the opportunity to *give* the gifts. It makes a lot of sense, don't you think?

You know, the world is an amazingly complex place. You can't figure it out in any meaningful sense. The only thing you have to pay attention to in your relationships—which can be richly complex, too—is *what's in it for you*. If you can always look at every situation in terms of what *you* can get out of it, *you* will be far, far ahead of the game.

Don't look at the relationship in terms of what you can do for your significant other. In fact, don't even think about the other as "significant" at all. What counts is what you get for yourself *out* of the other, and that keeps things at a simple, manageable level. If you were to express wild gratitude for what you got in the way of gifts or services, that would screw up everything. If you think of your relationship as a partnership where you owe as much as you get, that makes you tired just thinking about it.

Love isn't a partnership; it's an owner/owned situation . . . and you are definitely the owner.

10

♡ ♡ ♡ ♡

Compare Your Lover with Lovers You've Dated in the Past

Be sure to negatively compare your current lover with those you've had in the past in terms of lovemaking ability, generosity, power, looks, and connections. Don't compliment your current mate in any way. Instead, specifically point out what you miss about your last lover—how she looked like a *Penthouse* centerfold, how she stayed in bed with you for hours giving you more pleasure than you could have ever dreamed of—and wistfully recall just how indescribably delicious it all was. Just make sure your current girlfriend really knows how deficient she is based on the high standards that were set by those before her.

Now, you can really make this pay off big in terms of wrecking your love life if you combine two rules: Talk about how bad your current lover is, and do so in front of your friends. For instance, a good line is, "Suzy is such a killjoy. My old girlfriend, Delilah, liked to get really drunk, take off her blouse, and dance on the bar in her bra in front of the whole restaurant . . . but Suzy's a big dud."

It really doesn't matter *what* you say that compares your old lover with your new one. The whole point is that you want your lover to know in her heart that you're always secretly comparing her with someone else—and consistently finding something lacking. That inspires fear, resentment, loathing, and confusion, virtually guaranteeing an explosion of some sort, or at least severe depression somewhere down the pike. But do it anyway! Constantly keep your new gal in the insecure and hopeless maze of trying to live up to someone from your past.

And if she challenges you with, "Well, if your last girlfriend was so darned great, why aren't you with her now?" then just answer with raised eyebrows, or perhaps a slightly wistful look that implies, "Oh, how I wish I were!" That should set your lover back one or two paces, tee-hee.

11

♡♡♡♡

Talk about Yourself Exclusively

Suppose your lover calls you up in the middle of the workday to ask how you're feeling or just to share the communion of two loving souls. Well, don't buy it! You need to make it clear right from the start that the call is an excuse for you to talk ad nauseam about your latest problems with your co-worker or your boss or the woman who sells you bagels in the morning. Your points of view, what you have to complain about, what you have to brag about—that's all that matters. Don't let yourself get sucked into the silly idea that there should be any equality in the conversation or that you should actually show any real interest in your lover's issues. No, that would be insane.

Let's face it: It's really boring to listen to other people's problems. But for other people to hear *your* problems, now that's truly fascinating. Why is there a difference? Because *your* problems are about *you,* and that makes them far more interesting than what anybody else has to say.

Now, you may have heard that good listeners make good lovers. Or that good lovers are good listeners. Don't you believe it. Your lover's function is to be a good listener. *Your* function is to talk. And don't even slow down to hear a word about what's going on with him. Just let fly with all of your issues and concerns, and if he finds himself unable to listen any longer, just sulk in silence.

And by the way, you don't have to be original in your analysis of your problems. Feel totally free to repeat the same old stories and the same old grievances day after day, hour after hour. If your lover truly cares for you, those tales should be just as new and exciting to him the hundredth time as the first. Just talk and talk and talk, and then when you get bored, say you have to get off the phone.

This is your right. And if your lover says that it's urgent that you listen to him talk about some crisis of his, all you have to do is listen for a few seconds, then interrupt with, "Hey, that reminds me of what my sister did today. Can you believe her?!" And then launch into a diatribe of what your sister did to make you crazy.

Let your lover just stuff his feelings. It will do him good to realize that listening to you will enrich his life far more than talking ever could.

12

♡♡♡♡

Remember That Your Lover Is Your Punching Bag

We all have issues and crises that come up in the course of a day. That's normal, and it's just the way the world works. After all, it's frustrating and difficult to be a human being. We get dressed down by our bosses. We encounter bad drivers on the freeway. We often don't feel very well. We worry about money and mortality and weight. This is the natural course of life. And, just as naturally, this mortal life builds up anger and crises of the emotions and spirit. All of this means that we have to vent that anger and frustration somehow.

But how? We can't yell at our boss or we might get fired. We can't yell at our co-workers or we might get the reputation (however false!)

of being difficult to get along with. That might inhibit promotions or pay increases or might get us demoted. We can't just go out on the street and start screaming. This might get us locked up or shot (if we live in a place where unusual behavior leads to police shootings). We can't just start throwing our trash out on the street, even if it does mimic what we feel in our hearts.

So what do we do? Simple! We take it out on our lover! I mean, what was she put on the planet for except to be a punching bag, a bayonet practice dummy for our disappointments, worries, and fears? Yes! Get it in your head! Your lover exists to be screamed at and emotionally battered.

Suppose your boss reprimands you for screwing up a contract. Fair enough. This can happen at any time in the busy corporate world. Your task, after that happens, is to grin and bear it for the rest of the day, and then, when you get home, really let your mate have it. Take her to task over a messy kitchen or a leaky faucet or a joke that you didn't find funny, and just let it all out in any way you see fit. Remember, your lover is there to absorb your frustration with life like a sponge. If you know this and truly act on it, you'll feel a lot better. And who cares what kind of day she had? She's there for *you*, not the other way around. So when those bad days come around—and they will for all of us, due to health or finances or work or worry about the mortal condition—just bury it inside for a good long time, and then, whaaam, let it fly.

And if she threatens to call the police, be sure to whine and apologize and promise never to do it again—until the next time.

13

♡ ♡ ♡ ♡

Act Moody and Sulky when Your Lover Gets Home— but Don't Tell Him why You're Sulking!

Yes, that's it—keep him guessing! Make him play 20 questions! Keep him in a state of agony. Give monosyllabic answers or none at all when he asks you what's wrong. Just walk from room to room slamming doors. Be certain he knows nothing about why you're feeling the way you are. In fact, why not just sulk and be uncommunicative even if you're feeling fine. The idea is to keep your lover constantly off balance and make him wonder what's going on and what he did wrong. That way, you can keep him under your thumb even more than usual.

Look at it this way: It's your lover's job to guess what's on your mind, to be constantly appealing to you for clemency, to be humbled by your power. Part of that power consists of mystification, puzzlement, and bewilderment on his part. Use that power to keep him humbled. Act like a magician, and constantly hide what's going on beneath your hat so that your lover feels lost and confused all of the time, wondering what he might have done wrong to make you so unhappy.

Make sure he knows that it's his duty to be constantly on bended knee before your moods and contrariness, and that life will just continue like this forever. It's not as if you owe him any explanations—he should be able to read your mind and know exactly what's wrong with you!

14

♡♡♡♡

Remember That Your Lover Is Also Your Assistant, Lawyer, Placement Officer, Apartment Finder, and Loan Broker

Your lover isn't just there to help you with the little problems of life or to hold you tight on lonely nights. No, you see, your lover really *works for you!* She may have another job at some office or store or factory, true. But that's just a sideline. Her main job in life is to make your life easier.

For example, if she has a family friend or an "in" at a certain firm that she was counting on to help her get a new job, don't let her be selfish about it. That connection exists for *your* benefit, not hers! Or what if you need a new space to live and affordable apartments are hard to find? Well, then your lover simply has to spring into action. It's her duty to call all of her friends to help you find a place to live. And have her stay up all night doing it! Don't let her beg off because she's tired or sick—that's a sign of weakness, and it won't be tolerated. Remember, your lover works for *you,* and that means *all* the time, not just when she feels up to it. And, yes, the job includes lending you money without getting repaid.

She also needs to be right there providing you with legal and financial advice when required, and it's her duty to function as your personal assistant: That is, it's her responsibility to make your doctor and dentist appointments, to book your plane and restaurant reservations—basically anything you need done—and God forbid if she forgets to do something or flubs the job. Really let her have it. So what if you don't pay her for her services? She should be *happy* to work for you without pay. It's a privilege to make your life run smoothly!

This connects closely with the next crucial step in ruining your love life. . . .

15

♡ ♡ ♡ ♡

Don't for a Moment Let Your Lover Believe That He's Valued Just for Himself

Never let your lover think that for a minute. Far from it.

No! No! No! Never allow the slightest bit of complacency to enter his heart: He's valued for what he can do for *you*—and don't let him forget it! It's not about his fine character and how much he cares about you—it's about what he does for you in concrete, preferably economic, terms.

And certainly don't let your lover act as if he can get away with just being a great guy or gal without actually doing something *big* for you. For example, suppose your lover is one of the most decent, upstanding men in the community. Let's imagine that he owns a small factory and one of his employees does something really stupid at work. That employee brings his mobile home into the factory, then starts to do some welding work on the home. He works so carelessly that he starts a fire that destroys a good chunk of the plant. But your lover is such a great guy that he not only doesn't press charges or fire the worker, but he actually takes the fire-starting employee into his home and gives him a place to live—and even puts him in charge of rebuilding the factory!

Yeah? *So what good did that do for you?* So what if your lovers's a saint with other people? What has he done for *you* lately? What has he done that helps you get a new job or a new car or diamond jewelry?

Don't let him rest on his laurels and feel like a hero. Let him know that he has to do something concrete for you so his day will be complete. And you don't want to hear these nauseating feel-good stories about other people anyway. What a bunch of sappy treacle!

Here's another one: Let's say your lover has an elderly, somewhat confused father who's walking down the street at nighttime in dark clothes—on a rural road no less. A driver speeds around the corner, hits him, puts him in the hospital, and he dies a few days later. Your lover could raise hell and sue. Instead, he goes to the unlucky driver and tells her that the accident wasn't her fault. Then he totally forgives her and wishes her well. As a result, the entire community praises him for his forbearance.

Don't let these actions fool you for a minute. What on earth does all of this Good Samaritan behavior do for *you?*

Let your lover know the truth: He can't get away with these pitifully saintly acts when he's supposed to be taking care of you night and day! That, and that alone, is his job, and if he doesn't do it well enough, let him know it in no uncertain terms.

16

♡♡♡♡

Play Phone Games— That Is, Don't Return Her Calls So She Can See How Cool and Aloof You Are

There used to be a saying that went something like this: "No one was ever killed over the telephone." (It was said to me by a friend in high school.) But how wrong that is! You can wound and maim and torture and hound and hurt and maybe even kill as a result of your shenanigans over the phone. You can do the obvious: not return calls and make your lover crazy. You can make her beg and plead to have you return the call. You can be even more clever:

You can make her absolutely insane by letting her make several phone calls, while you make one call at some odd time that keeps her from possibly responding to it—and then have her make ten more calls that you don't answer at all.

Now, I, your humble servant, know very well that you might be saying to yourself, "Hey, that sounds like junior high school stuff. Aren't we supposed to be more mature than that?" No! *Love is a junior high school game!* If you acknowledge that right now, then you know a lot more than most people—and you certainly know more about how to ruin your love life than your lover or any of your "friends."

Another phone game you can play is a lot of fun: When your lover has just about had it and is about to jump off a bridge, you can just nonchalantly call as if nothing's happened, and if she asks where the heck you've been, just say, "Oh, I've been busy at work," and don't say any more about it! Tee-hee!

The phone-game rule is really a lot more cunning than it sounds, because it epitomizes the essence of a screwed-up love relationship: taking a potentially adult, mature union to the level of a seventh-grade competition to see who can get the better of the other. Try it, and you'll be amazed at how well it works.

Maybe human beings can't be killed over the telephone, as my childhood friend Marvin reminded me 44 years ago—but relationships surely can be.

17

♡♡♡♡

Make Fun of Your Lover's Family

To you, maybe, your family is sacrosanct. Your parents are the ones who gave you birth and sustained you, and despite your occasional anger and frustration with them, you love them a lot. You would certainly not take kindly to anyone mocking them. This is all very well and good and totally understandable. But the fact that your family is precious to you doesn't mean a thing when it comes to belittling the members of your *lover's* family.

Have they failed to show you due deference and respect in every situation? Have they neglected to behave as if you were a god? Have they ever put any other interest ahead of you?

Have they ever been less than prompt about serving you your meals when you came over to their house? Have they ever talked about themselves before they inquired about you? If so, then don't spare the sarcasm and cruelty.

Off with their heads! Show them no mercy whatsoever. They've behaved abominably, and don't hesitate to let your lover know it.

Did his parents fail to get you the gift you wanted for your birthday or Christmas or Hanukkah or Kwanzaa? Then they surely deserve to have you skewer them unmercifully every time their names are brought up. Or put it like this: Have they ever failed to acknowledge that their son is unbelievably, phenomenally lucky to have you in his miserable life? Then they deserve to be criticized unmercifully.

In fact, why wait for a special occasion? Why not just make cruel fun of them anytime it comes into your head to say anything at all? Why not make it a staple of your dialogue with your lover to mock and belittle his family—especially his mother and father—whenever you can squeeze it in?

Now, your lover may wince and protest. But that just shows that it's time to invoke an earlier rule and start belittling him for being a mama's boy. That's right—make him feel even worse than he already does!

Don't hold back when it comes to discussion of brothers or sisters either. It's true that some people feel an unbreakable bond with their siblings, and this may, in fact, apply to you. Perhaps your big brother rescued you from some mean kids on the playground when you were a tyke, or your sister once gave you $100 so you could buy a new outfit for the school dance. Whatever the case, you might very well feel extremely attached to your kin. And that's just fine.

But when it comes to your lover's siblings, that's a whole different kettle of fish. Those brothers or sisters exist solely for your belittlement. Mock their accents. Show contempt for their achievements or lack of them. Point out their failings, and here it doesn't matter if the failings are real or imagined. Just make a case for whatever's wrong with them, and you can be certain that your lover will just bow his head and take it. I've said it before and I'll say it again: Do not treat your lover the way you want to be treated (excuse me, *demand* to be treated!). For heaven's sake, treat him like the doormat he is. (After all, what other kind of human being would have you, but let's keep that little secret to ourselves!)

So, feel no compunction whatsoever about treating your lover's family to a daily roasting—in front of your lover and whoever else is available to listen.

Good, that's settled.

18

♡♡♡♡

Let It Be Known That You Consider Affection to Be a Chore

Yes, this one's a killer! Make sure that your lover knows very well that you would rather do almost anything else than hug her, kiss her, or make love to her.

Of course, if you feel like it, you'll *do it*. At least, occasionally. But that doesn't mean you have to *like* doing it.

"All right, all right," you'll say with a sigh, "I guess we can make love, but we'll have to make it fast because I have an early meeting in the morning."

Or, try this: "Really? But didn't we just do it a week or two ago?" Or "Aww, I sort of felt like having a drink and watching *Jimmy Kimmel Live* instead. But if you insist, let's get it over with." Or "Well, all right. But I do have this rash. . . ."

Let your lover know beyond any shadow of a doubt that affection isn't something you crave because you're having loving feelings or just want to feel the closeness that having sex with your mate brings. Instead, act as if affection is just a gift that you'll grant—on special occasions—to your lover out of a sense of *noblesse oblige* and not out of any need for intimacy.

This one is a perfect, shimmering gem. It keeps your lover off balance—as so many of these suggestions do—and makes certain that she knows that she's on a short leash, is way near the end of that leash, and you can jerk it back to catch her up in a noose of low self-esteem at any time.

Affection—that is, physical affection—is basic to relationships in most cases. To make sure your lover knows you grant it only grudgingly and at your own sweet discretion is an ideal way to keep the relationship on consistently uncertain and uneasy terms.

So starting right now, keep her writhing in confusion and doubt so that you'll truly have the upper hand!

Now, this one is so important that I think I might even italicize it. Yes, I think I will, actually:

19

♡♡♡♡

If You're Dating Someone Who Has a Lot of Problems, Is Generally a Mess, and All of Your Friends Dislike Him, Get Married Anyway— Marriage Will Cure All of Your Problems!

Now it may be true that you've heard just the opposite—that is, that marrying someone with a lot of problems is a recipe for disaster because his problems will only continue and probably even get worse in the hothouse atmosphere of marriage. You may have heard that people don't change once they get married, and you'll just be locked in legally to someone with a lot of baggage.

Nonsense! The moment the minister, priest, rabbi, or justice of the peace says, "I now pronounce you husband and wife," all of your lover's flaws and problems will vanish like the mist off Malibu Beach after lunch. You won't have any more problems with his lying or drinking. No. You'll never again have to deal with his laziness and refusal to get a job. And you won't have to worry about his propensity for reckless spending, gambling, cheating, and occasional stealing (from your wallet). Absolutely not. From the moment you say "I do," your mate will suddenly become a perfect, divine being with stellar character.

And how does this miracle occur, you might ask? *Because, you see, marriage changes people so completely that they become model citizens in an instant.*

Now, it's conceivable that even *you* have some flaws, or at least some doubts about yourself and your abilities to be a good marriage partner. It doesn't matter—get married anyway!

All of your problems and self-doubt will vanish into nothingness if you believe in the marriage fairy. Count on the magical powers inherent in reciting those marriage vows (and having a really expensive wedding that puts your parents into debt for years) and you'll be *saved* (no evangelist needed)!

Just remember: Whatever your issues, whatever your mate's issues, marry anyway! That's a sure way to wreck your love life, so go ahead and do it now.

20

♡♡♡♡

Don't Ever Tell Your Lover, "I Love You"

Why should you utter those three insignificant words? Don't you have any short-term memory? I just told you a few pages back that love was a junior high school game. Why didn't you believe me?

What that meant was that although your lover is expected to constantly tell *you* that she loves you, you never have to reply in kind. Make her pant for it. Make her beg (similar to stingily doling out affection)! Make her yearn desperately for even a hint of "I love you." Yes, it's true that it gives you a certain amount of satisfaction to hear your lover say she adores you. There's something rather pleasurable about getting e-mails at work that close with a loving sentiment. But that doesn't mean you have to do anything in return, any more than you have to return phone calls promptly.

Repeat after me: Love is a junior high school game if you really want to do it well (and cruelly). So spare those three little words . . . and spoil the relationship.

21

♡ ♡ ♡ ♡

Have a Relationship with Someone Who's Never Happy and Is Always Down in the Dumps . . . and Believe You Can Change Him and Make Him Happy

Yes, you may have heard that someone who's really down, gloomy, and angry all the time is doomed to stay that way. But that's not necessarily true in your case. *You* can change your lover simply by being in a relationship with him.

Now, this bit of advice is a little different from some of the previous rules. Usually, I tell you how to jam the other person's gears and make yourself the master. But in just this one case, let's reverse things a bit.

You see, in this situation, your lover is making you miserable on a consistent basis by engaging in many of the steps I've delineated up to this point. He's berating you, cheating on you, lying, being disrespectful, and disparaging your friends and family. Now a reasonable person might have seen this coming on when consistently faced with a grumpy, mean-spirited individual. But no, not *you!* You're convinced that you *will* change him and make him into a happy, chirpy little angel of light. You can be sure of it. Yes, maybe no one else can do it, but you can! You can actually change human personality just by being in his presence, and make him happy although there's no evidence that he's ever felt that emotion a day in his life.

Don't be swayed by naysayers, though. No, Pollyanna, just dedicate yourself to doing everything you can for your lover—although you're miserable all the while—and I promise that you'll be a happy, happy camper for the rest of your days.

(Yeah, right.)

Now, back to driving your lover crazy instead of driving yourself crazy . . .

22

♡♡♡♡

Expect Your Lover to Look like Someone Out of a <u>Penthouse</u> Centerfold

Don't for a minute let your lover off the hook when it comes to appearance. That's right. *You* can gain as much weight as you want and sport long, shaggy, goofy-looking hair. But make sure she knows that you expect her to look fabulous at all times. She has to diet, work out, have plastic surgery, dye her hair—basically do anything and everything to keep up the facade. And you don't have to do anything but sit back and criticize!

That's your prerogative. Just be certain to really stay on top of the situation. Maybe tack up sample diets and exercise programs on the refrigerator door, or give her articles to read that you find in magazines such as *Shape* and *Self* about makeovers and liposuction. And don't forget to tack centerfolds from *Playboy* or *Penthouse* in the den or bathroom to show her just how inadequate she is. Also be sure to bring up the subject of friends or acquaintances who used to be ". . . you know, obese, like you . . ." and got themselves straightened out by some superhuman feat of self-discipline—or maybe by having their intestines stapled.

You can be confident that your lover will be happy to be frequently told how she can perfect her appearance. People like to be reminded of their flaws—especially by their lovers. And don't forget to pinch her upper arm or her thigh every once in a while to remind her that she's got extra fat in those areas—everyone loves that!

By letting your lover know that you think she could be perfected in some very basic ways, she'll realize how incredibly lucky she is that you tolerate her. She'll feel permanently ill at ease, knowing that on any given day you might dump her for someone who's better looking. People really like that feeling of insecurity and of not being loved for themselves.

And one last thing to remember: Your lover, as noted previously, is a punching bag for you, so if you happen to feel some insecurity about your own appearance, why not take it out on her? (After all, this could inspire her to have plastic surgery on her nose, which she could really use!)

That makes sense, doesn't it? Make *her* feel bad all the time so you don't have to. You'll both be a lot happier.

23

♡♡♡♡

Feel Free to Say Any Cruel Thing You Want to Your Lover, and When Reproached about It, Say, "Hey, Can't I Even Express My <u>Feelings?</u>"

Yes, actually say *"feelings"* in a reverential way so that your lover knows that once the word is invoked, you can say anything you want and get away with it. When you're in the midst of voicing these all-important thoughts, nothing else can possibly be allowed to come in the way of that expression. Saying how you feel is as basic as breathing in and out, right? If your lover doesn't allow you to express those feelings, isn't he suffocating you? Of course he is!

So say anything you like—no matter how hurtful—and when your lover says, "That's a bit rude, isn't it?" respond with an outraged look and a haughty reply, such as: "Oh, I guess I'm not allowed to say anything at all, right? From now on, I'll just talk to my cat. She lets me say anything I want and doesn't jump down my throat."

Or else, say something really cutting, maybe about his mother or father, and then when he looks shocked, say, "I'm just trying to have a healthy relationship by expressing my feelings. But I guess that's not allowed. What am I supposed to do—keep it all bottled up inside me forever?! I don't think that would be healthy for either of us, do *you?*"

The beauty of this is that your lover really can't provide an adequate response to your "logic." What's he going to say—"No, you're not *allowed* to express your feelings"? Of course not.

So, feel free to say or even do anything you want, and know you can get away with it. Why? Well, shucks, you're just expressing your feelings.

24

♡♡♡♡

Forbid Your Lover to See Her Friends

Now, you may have heard some balderdash to the effect that friends are even more important than family, that friends are the family members we choose for ourselves. And, yes, maybe that's true. Some people can be extremely attached to their friends. I would imagine that you, dear reader, are very attached to yours and might even become hysterical with shock, rage, and frustration if anyone tried to keep you from seeing them.

But that's *you*—and *your* feelings count for a heck of a lot more than anyone else's. In fact, they count for everything, and that's precisely why you should feel free to forbid your lover from seeing her friends. It's entirely possible that many of her friends were on board before she met you, so by virtue of seniority, those friends might even believe that they have an equitable claim on your lover's time and attention. Those "friends" (put it in quotes, because what do they count for compared with you?) might even feel that they have a right to criticize and judge you! You heard me right. They might feel that way because they've known your lover since infancy or grade school. Well, that's just plain intolerable.

If you catch even a whiff of such freaking treason (and *treason* is not too strong a word here), you must nip it in the bud right away by simply telling your lover that she's no longer allowed to visit with Bonnie or Karen or whoever it may be. If she starts to pull a long face and sulk, you can just nail her good by screaming that if she wants to associate with people who are trying to sabotage your relationship, you might as well call it quits right then and there!

Now, it would bother you a lot if your lover tried to pull the same thing with you, but as my pal, the eminent investor and shrink, Phil DeMuth, says, "That's someone else's feelings, and only your feelings count." So just steamroll right over your lover's objections, and make sure to control the access she has to any negative input—or even questionable input—about you.

Your goal here is to basically put your lover in a situation similar to that of a person living in a totalitarian state. That level of control will basically make your lover's life easier. She doesn't need to have any discretion or independence of mind. You can start making all of her decisions by just regulating who her friends are and when they can be in her presence. You know what? She'll get used to it. And she'll even thank you eventually—because, hey, you're the boss!

Now, I want to shift gears a tiny bit here. So far, most of this book has been about how to ruin your love life, assuming you already have a relationship that can be ruined. That's well and good, and we all need this advice. But how about some advice for those of you who don't have a relationship yet? How about some tips that will ensure that you will never have a decent relationship—not even for a few months? I, your faithful author, certainly don't want any of you who are not in a relationship to feel as if you're being slighted. So please read on for some advice on how to make sure you never have the chance to develop any kind of decent love life in the first place.

25

♡ ♡ ♡ ♡

Only Pursue Men or Women Who Are Already Taken

Sometimes the best, most powerful advice is the simplest, and that's certainly the case here. How can you make sure that you have the smallest possible chance of actually having a decent love life? Simple, silly: Choose someone who's already married or dating someone else! This will more or less guarantee that you'll have an truly unsatisfactory love life. (I exclude those who are legally married but are in fact separated—let's forget about them for this discussion.)

If you think about it, you'll realize that many of the world's most charming men and women are already hitched. They're often far more delightful to be around than those who are single. But if they're married, you can only be with them for fleeting moments. So they'll truly help you attain your goal of ruining your love life by making sure it's always unsatisfying and lacking in substance.

You might also find it worthwhile to try "dating" someone who's gay and only attracted romantically to his own sex. Once again, these individuals can be thoroughly delightful. And they're often quite good-looking. So go ahead and fall in love with a homosexual if you're a heterosexual (or vice versa). The result is almost sure to be a maddening period of frustration and loneliness.

Similarly, why not develop a relationship with someone who's a hopeless workaholic? This isn't as bad as dating someone who's married, but it comes close. The workaholic is married to his *work,* and his relations with anyone and anything *but* his work will always be of a meager and unsatisfying kind. You may very well get him to the altar . . . but that may also be the last you see of him for some time to come.

Or try dating someone who's unavailable because he's still basically having a romantic relationship with his mother or father. There are plenty of these folks around, and you may manage to corral one of them to the altar. But you're going to be stunned by just how little real devotion you get out of this species when push comes to shove and the time for choosing between Mom and Dad on the one hand, and you on the other, comes up.

To be sure, devotion to one's parents is a fine thing, noble and pure. But dating someone in his 20s or 30s or (heaven forbid) older, who still lives with Mom and Pop—well, good luck to you. You're looking for fish in a desert.

There are undoubtedly countless other ways in which people can be unavailable to you— both emotionally and physically (how about falling for a Catholic priest!), and I couldn't possibly list them all here. But the general principle should suffice: If you want to have a relationship that's guaranteed to fail, definitely pursue someone who's already taken!

26

♡ ♡ ♡ ♡

Always Look Your Worst— or at Any Rate, Don't Bother to Look Your Best

Perhaps you've heard the ancient piece of wisdom that "love enters through the eyes . . ." This just implies that men and women fall in love because they like the way the other person looks. And certainly, there's a multimillion-dollar industry in this country alone that says that we should all look our best—the intent being to impress and attract the opposite (or maybe the same) sex.

Men and women go to gyms, sweat, struggle, and torture themselves—all to tone their bodies to optimal fitness. Similarly, people diet, starve themselves, have surgery, buy prodigious amounts of makeup, and purchase the latest fashions—all to make themselves look wonderfully attractive and sexy (at least to themselves).

Well, love comes in through the eyes all right; and the human race, even in the most dire straits of illness, poverty, and war, will always take the time to look good. It's a basic part of the condition of all living creatures (including plants and animals), who go to a lot of genetically engineered effort to look their best to attract mates and continue the species.

But none of this means a thing to you! You can and must look any old way you feel like. It's a law set down in the Commandments that you must only do what's easiest and requires the least effort on your part—and to hell with what other people think. Let your hair be unkempt and greasy. Get fat. Wear dirty clothes. In fact, go to a lot of trouble to make yourself look positively unsightly—not just ordinary, but ugly. Tattoo your entire body. Put hooks and other metal in your face and call it face jewelry. Make yourself look absolutely hideous with this stuff, and call it fashion.

And don't make it easy for the world to *see* the real you. Make them really stretch and struggle to find out just who you are. And don't bother to help them by advertising yourself as attractive. Instead, put your ugly face forward and make them search for that really lovely person who's presumably hidden under the grunge and sweat stains and pimples and grease (the alternative, of course, is that the hideous one *is* the real you, but that's just not possible, is it?).

Those fashion magazines don't know what they're talking about. You can be just as slobby as you want and the world will owe it to you to find the real you. Yes, the world commands that every other human look great and go to a lot of trouble just to get a second glance. But *you* don't have to. In your case, the world will make an exception and like you even better . . . the worse you look.

27

♡♡♡♡

Be Consistently Surly and Unfriendly

This one is so basic that maybe it should be set in glowing neon letters. If the publishers can't arrange that, then just take my word for it—this is the big one, the nuclear bomb of ways to ruin your love life by making sure you don't have one to start with.

You may have noticed that from elementary school—no, from kindergarten—onward, the kids who had girlfriends and boyfriends tended to be the ones who were friendly, outgoing, and pleasant. And in adult life, it's nearly universally true that those who have friends and lovers are the ones who have some manners and are able to make conversation, express some interest in others, and have what we might call a civilized approach to life.

You may have even heard that men and women often make friends first before becoming lovers. This surely is a basic fact of human existence for most people: The friendlier and easier to get along with you are, the better the chance that you'll find a wonderful person who can be your lover.

Yes, this is true for the human race—and even for dogs, cats, and other cute and furry species. But it isn't going to be true for *you*. You can act just as rude and surly as you want. You can be reclusive and unpleasant. You can punctuate your speech with sarcasm and anger. You can stand mute when asked even the most innocuous questions and simply respond with a look of contempt and derision.

And when you behave in this rude way, it's the other person's duty to work through your defenses and your rudeness to find the lovely invisible self that might possibly be lurking beneath all the barbs and thorns.

You say that you're 40 and you've been doing this rude act all of your life and no one has yet bothered to try to penetrate it? Well, then act even ruder. The problem might just be that you're being too nice even though you're not trying to be.

Stand up for yourself! Make it really, really hard for anyone to be your friend or lover. Put up barbed wire. Build minefields. It's the world's duty to get through all of that to find the charming inner you that might (or might not) be lurking there.

Just be sure that you never act friendly, nice, kind, or compassionate—and your love life will take care of itself.

28

♡♡♡♡

Act Like a Big Baby on Dates

Looking slobby and acting surly should prevent you from having that date in the first place. But let's suppose that someone really does go to the trouble of trying to get through to you. Furthermore, let's say that you get asked out, either on a date or as part of a group, and then you split off with someone who seems to be particularly interested in you.

To make sure that your love life *stays* ruined, act like a big baby on your date by doing all or some of the following:

— *Talk nonstop, and talk only about yourself.* This, by the way, is darned good advice for wrecking any situation, but it's especially good for wrecking a date. Don't ask any questions of your companion. Don't talk about movies or music or art or world affairs. Don't ask her where she's from, where she went to college, what she does for a living, or whether she has any brothers and sisters. Only talk about yourself (without letting her get a word in edgewise, of course), and by all means resist any attempts by your companion to interject discussion on some topic she's interested in. Talk until her eyes glaze over. Talk until all the servers at the restaurant have gone home. Talk like there's no tomorrow. Just talk, talk, talk—and don't listen to one damn thing she has to say! I'll say it over and over: Talk only about yourself, you big lovable ogre.

— *Bitch and complain.* Don't ever say anything positive. Bitch and moan about your work. Whine about your parents. Complain bitterly about your neighbors. Bitch about politics and about the economy. Make sure the person you're with knows that you have a totally dour attitude about life. It will do you a lot of good to always appear down, gloomy, and unsatisfied. People enjoy being around others who are really depressed. So act as glum as you can.

And it's really crucial that you talk nonstop about your health—or lack thereof. Go into excruciating detail about your illnesses—especially reproductive- and digestive-system conditions. Talk about that gross scar running across your abdomen, and oh, don't forget your persistent problem with flatulence. Maybe even provide sound effects. Explain how you don't really need a lover so much as a nurse or doctor. People who barely know you will really want to hear about your diseases, your operations, and your medications. So just talk about all of this as much as possible right off the bat—and you're sure to get a good-night kiss (off).

— *Brag wildly, while at the same time maintaining a completely negative attitude about life.* Tell her how many triumphs you've had at work—or would have if the system wasn't stacked against you. Boast about how cool your comeback was to your boss—until he fired you. Talk about what a great-looking family you come from—except that everyone needed to have plastic surgery to achieve that look.

Bragging is a big way to guarantee that the other person you're with will absolutely never want to see you again. So do it, and be happy with yourself. But if you *are* happy with yourself, act unhappy. Understand? But then you're never happy, so never mind.

— *Go on and on about old lovers.* This is so important that it's worth repeating. I know I already hinted at this earlier in the part about how to ruin existing love relationships. And believe me, it works. But it works just as well if you're trying to ensure that you never have a relationship at all. I'm not going to belabor such a lovely and beguiling point. Let's just say, "Try it. You'll like it." Talk about previous lovers right from the start, and you'll find that you eventually have absolutely no one else to talk to at all.

— *Make alcohol and/or drugs the third partner at each and every social interaction. In fact, show up drunk or stoned for your first date.* If your date indignantly points out that you're intoxicated, just tell her that she should have a few drinks or take a few hits on the bong, too, because "it'll loosen you up." Then, when you go out on your date, get steadily drunker. Or more stoned. This is a certified, dyed-in-the-wool showstopper. Hardly any date can survive if the participants are whacked. Being drunk or stoned leads to lousy interpersonal relationships, arguments, long pauses, uncontrolled giggling, shameless flirting with strangers—virtually a whole special category of ruinous relationship patterns (including, of course, risking killing someone while you're on your date by driving drunk or stoned!).

And here's a very important point: Don't just reserve alcohol and drugs for new beginnings in dating and relationships. Make sure you're drunk or high every time you see or even talk to your lover. Continual inebriation is one of the best ways to wreck even the hardiest of relationships, as the partakers slip into comas of self-obsession, unreality, and obnoxiousness. Count on it. So, make alcohol and drugs your constant companions. It'll work like a charm.

Now let's assume that you followed all of the great advice offered above and did your best to nip the relationship in the bud, but it still didn't work and you somehow managed to start up a relationship.

If that's the case, here are some more suggestions for how to ruin it pronto. . .

29

♡♡♡♡

Take Total Possession of Your Lover's Home

Make sure that your lover knows that you're now in residence and in charge.

If you're a man, leave your clothes around the apartment, and also camp out in the bathroom reading the sports page of *The Times*. If you're a woman, after you've spent a night or two at the apartment of your new lover, leave panties and a big box of Tampax lying around.

Be rude to her friends. Redecorate his place without asking. Eat everything that's in her refrigerator and don't replace it for her. Read his snail mail *and* his e-mail behind his back. Rummage through her closets and drawers. Answer his phone and act really rude to whoever calls—especially if it's his parents. If they seem a bit shocked that a stranger is answering the phone, make lewd innuendoes about the sex you had the night before. Change the message on the machine so that you're on it, either in the background or actually on the outgoing message.

Just assume that your lover's house is now yours, and that you can do any old thing you want in it. Show him who's boss by planting the flag of your possessions in his dwelling. Intrude on the peace and quiet of her home by blasting loud music and by inviting your obnoxious, raucous friends over without asking her.

Remember, your lover's place is now yours (and don't forget to make copies of his keys behind his back). People like to be violated and pushed around in their own personal space, and this will do very well for you. It virtually guarantees a swift end to the relationship (which is what you want, right?).

30

♡♡♡♡

Flirt with Anyone and Everyone— in Front of Your Lover

This is so important that it not only applies to the folks *in* a relationship, but also to those who might be contemplating getting into one, are just starting one, or who are going out on a first date.

First and foremost, flirt with your date's roommate. Yes! Yes! Yessss! Even as your date is getting ready for you, engage in sexual innuendo with the person she lives with—preferably within your date's earshot. And then once you're out on the date, turn up the flirt-a-thon meter. Flirt with the valet parking attendant. Flirt with the other person's date if you're doubling. Engage in a long conversation with the restaurant hostess, delving into where she's from, what her real job is, how she got to be so cute, and in the meantime, completely ignore your date. Show much more warmth to an old girlfriend you run into than you do to the person you're actually having dinner with.

When you go to the movies, flirt with the gal behind you in line. And then, when your date's in the middle of a sentence, make a big show of turning your head to stare at the good-looking babe who just walked by. Flirt with any and every woman who crosses your path!

Short of having sex with someone else right in front of your date, there's practically nothing else you can do to wound her feelings as deeply and as consistently as flirting with others. It goes right to the core of any relationship and can ruin it immediately. Or even better, it will slowly eat away at it like battery acid for days, weeks, and months (c'mon, no one taking these rules seriously will have a relationship that lasts beyond months!). Flirting with others belittles your lover, makes her feel jealous and insignificant, and keeps her in a state of perpetual anger.

Bottom line: You can't lose in the relationship-killing department by flirting constantly with others in front of your lover. Flirting: It's to relationships what atom bombs are to cities.

31

♡ ♡ ♡ ♡

Make the Decision That You're Going to Marry for Money— and Don't Let Love Enter into the Equation

You may have heard the old saw that the hardest way on earth to earn money is to marry it. That is, you have to kowtow to your spouse's rich family; you have to tolerate their automatic assumption that they're better than you are because their bank account has more zeroes at the end of it, and you have to figure out which fork to use when sitting at their lavish dinner table.

Well, that's all nonsense. Rich people are very friendly and tolerant of poor people who are courting their son or daughter just for their money. They'll love the thought that they're going to be sharing their money with someone who doesn't have a dime. And they'll treat you nicely and even dote on you simply because you're *not* rich.

Yes, and if you believe that, I have an Internet stock to sell you.

The sadder truth just might be that the wealthy will in fact treat you like dirt because *they* are rich and *you* are poor, and this is a fact of life, not to be changed or tampered with by you or anyone else. Rich people want their kids to marry other rich people's kids. The famous phrase, "Rich marries rich," happens to be true, and if you try to tamper with it, you cross an invisible but very painful line of demarcation that will shock you out of your misconceptions.

So go ahead. Do everything possible to marry someone just for money—not for love or contentment or lifelong enjoyment—and I'll guarantee that your life will be rich . . . in misery.

32

♡♡♡

If Your Lover Has Parents who Are Simply Intolerable, Believe in Your Heart That He or She will Turn Out Totally—or Even a Little Bit—Different from Those Parents

You've probably heard people say that if you want to get a good idea of what your lover is going to look like in 30 years or so, have a gander at her parents. You'll get an eyeful. But there's something much deeper level that you might want to think about. That is, if you want to assess what your lover's personality is going to be like, check out how her parents or older siblings act *now.*

Rarely in this world does the apple fall very far from the tree, and it's not likely that it will in this case either. If you're a man and your lover's mother is materialistic, carping, and complaining, but your lover is a flower child, think about it: Her mother is not going to change into a flower child. But your lover may very well change into Mom—and that's a scary prospect indeed.

If you're a woman and your lover is a robust, hearty sportsman, and his father is a complaining, racist old alcoholic, you may well find that as time goes by, your lover gets to be far more like his father than is comfortable.

If you make your choice based on the firm conviction that your lover will never change, will always be as wonderful as she is now, and will never fall into the gravity of her parents' behavior, you're an astounding optimist, to put it mildly.

But knowing you and how everything always works out for you, you'll probably just go ahead and marry the man or woman with the monsters-from-hell parents. In your case, and *only* in your case, will the apple actually fall *far* from the tree. Good luck!

33

♡♡♡♡

Act Out of Jealousy Any Old Time You Feel Like It; In Fact, Let Jealousy Rule Your Life

You've probably noticed that people don't always make the best decisions when they're motivated by jealousy. In fact, it's almost impossible to think clearly when you're getting whipped around by this most insatiable and evil of personality demons. Jealousy can make even the most sensible woman go berserk, and can make even the most calm of men go shrieking insane.

But don't let that stop you in the slightest in your quest to totally control your lover with this emotion. You're the only person in history who will make the proper decisions while under the influence of the green-eyed monster. You and you alone can make the envy devil your god and still make things work for you.

For example, did you see him talking to another woman in a department store—not in a flirtatious way, but just transacting business? Did you see her smiling warmly to a client as she tried to close the sale of a house?

Freak out! Go crazy on her. Start yelling at him. Throw major fits. Go totally insane with rage (always a good idea when trying to annihilate any relationship anyway). Toss dishes around. Slam doors. Run out the door and swear you're never coming back.

Did you happen to come upon some ten-year-old photos of your lover with an old girlfriend? *Go berserk!* Make him writhe and bend and break with his own hysteria as he cowers from your rage. Spare no wrath. That's for wimps and losers. Pour on all of the fury until you feel as if the blood vessels in your forehead are about to burst.

This is the way to make sure you're absolutely and totally in control—let your own emotions run wild, and trample on the dignity and self-esteem of your lover on a continual basis.

Be sure he knows it's your way—with your hysterical fits of jealousy that can flare up at any time—or the highway. I assure you that things will work out just as you would think.

Bye-bye, love.

34

♡♡♡♡

Trust That First Flush of Love, Affection, and Sexual Excitement— and <u>Know</u> That It Will Last Forever

In that warm glow at 4 A.M., after three bouts of lovemaking, when you're still bursting with excitement that she actually came home with you—that's the time to make long-term plans. Although you've never ended up in a relationship with someone you made love to on the first night you met, you know that *this* time it will be different. In fact, this will probably last forever. So make her a key to your apartment and lend her some money—after all, you'll probably end up marrying this person. Yes, you can bask in that warm glow after your first few episodes of love, and know that this is the woman who will bear your children or the man who will care for you in your old age.

You can have faith in that first blast of fireworks. It will light up the sky of your love forever, and your dazzling opinion of your lover will never change. After all, the more you know about people, the more you admire them—isn't that the way it works? And don't lovers always look better in the morning?

This is so obvious that I think I'll just let it go at that.

•

35

♡♡♡♡

Develop an Intense Relationship with Someone with Severe Personal Problems, and Believe in Your Heart That You Can Change Him

That's right. If your lover has mind-blowing personal problems that seem to be totally unfixable, don't worry. *You* can fix those problems. You and you alone can change human personality so that your lover becomes more honest, more caring, more selfless. You have that magic power that only genies usually have to alter people's behavior. You'll be just as powerful as Jahweh was with Moses near the burning bush. You'll be the lightning bolt in his life that changes him into exactly the person you want him to be.

In fact, this leads to an equally powerful rule: If you start a relationship with someone who has horrific problems, continue with that relationship indefinitely, because he'll most certainly change into the person you want him to be *in time.* Don't give up. Just stay with the loser forever, and he will eventually—through the chemical magic of your strong personality—become a shining star.

Is he a liar? So what? *You* will turn him into the next George Washington. Is he a shirker and a slacker? Never mind. Your relentless nagging will transform him into Bill Gates. Is he constantly unfaithful? So what. If you stay with him forever and devote your life to that cause, maybe by the time you're 70 he'll understand the concept of fidelity.

Remember, people do change—but only for you—and only if you love them with all your heart.

36

♡ ♡ ♡ ♡

Have an Affair with Your Lover's Best Friend or Roommate, and Trust That She'll Never Find Out or Even Care!

You know she's been eyeing you. Go for it! Flirt with her, then get her drunk and have sex with her. Your girlfriend won't find out. No way. She'll just go on with her life and work and will probably be too preoccupied to even care when her roommate comes into her room and says, "I have a terrible confession to make. I'm so sorry. Boo-hoo."

And then, when the confession about your making tacos together is out in the open, your lover will just casually tell her roommate (with a smile), "Oh, that Johnny, he's a wild man. He's totally insane. What a character. Listen, I have a lot of work to do. Could you leave me alone for a while?" (While she gets out the butcher's knife.) No, really, lovers don't care if you have sex with their best friends. Just go ahead and do it (I mean, "do" *her*) and live it up while you're at it.

You and you alone can betray your lover with someone close to her and get away with it. Go ahead! Live dangerously! Have a good time. It'll be something you can tell your grandchildren. People like to be surprised by things that will jolt them to their very core.

So just go for it, have a great time, and you'll soon be having fun and laughing like mad with your lover once again—money-back guarantee (you've heard about Winning Ben Stein's Money, right?).

37

♡♡♡♡

Pretend to Be Someone You're Not

Pretend to be rich if you're poor. Pretend to be socially prominent even if you're a nobody. Pretend to be a total superstar, and keep up the illusion as long as you possibly can.

Pretend you're tough when you're weak. Pretend you're a filmmaker when you're a sales clerk. Just pretend constantly, and soon enough, it will all work out, and you'll be in hog heaven, pretending to be what you're not even a little bit.

Your lover will delight in discovering that the person she's dating is a total phony. She'll love finding out that the guy she's been spending the night with has been telling big fat lies about who he is.

Some might say it undermines the basis of the relationship when someone constantly lies. But that's nonsense. Why? Because when you make up a totally phony persona for yourself, it shows how imaginative and clever you are to have been able to keep up that lie for so long. It shows that you're really a magician who can shape reality in whatever way you choose. What an amazing talent!

Don't buy into that b.s. about how people don't like to be lied to. You can do any old thing you want any old time you want and get away with it, as long as you're charming in your wildly amusing duplicity.

38

♡ ♡ ♡ ♡

Get Involved in Your Lover's Family Business

You heard me right. Insinuate yourself into your lover's family business as thoroughly and as quickly as possible. Don't worry that this will create problems and complications that you couldn't have even conceived of. Just get a big bowl and toss in jealousy, competition, financial conflicts, personality quirks, and family secrets—and watch that old pot boil. What fun you'll have!

Some may say that things might erupt because other employees (or family members) will be jealous of you, and maybe they'll be suspicious that you won't have to work as hard as everyone else, but that's silly. Some might also say that there will inevitably be a problem if you combine the intricacies of (future or current) in-laws, work, and love together. But that's nonsense, too. No, you will be able to make it all work. So just embroil yourself in the inner business workings of your lover's family—and see what happens! Chances are, you'll end up with one very happy soufflé of good cheer, insouciance, and lifelong prosperity.

And the French are our best friends!

39

♡♡♡♡

Believe in Your Heart That There's Always Someone Better Just Around the Corner, and Treat Your Current Lover Like He or She Is Merely a Temporary Substitute for the Real Thing

If you're a woman, steal a look at your current lover. Is he as good-looking as Brad Pitt? As muscular as Arnold? As smart as your most erudite college professor? As rich as a Rockefeller?

If you're a man, is she as lovely as Ashley Judd? As well paid as Oprah Winfrey? As sexy as Nicole Kidman? If you answer in the negative, then why the heck are you bothering with this person? All you have to do is keep in mind that your current lover can and will be replaced at the drop of a hat by someone else who might be sexier, richer, better connected, and have a better figure.

Always express reservations about your lover, too, and never commit fully—because you know that there's someone much better right around the bend. By keeping your lover guessing, you can ensure that he'll also be in that fragile state of insecurity that will keep him on his toes. And you'll also want to be on *your* toes—so that you're ready to pounce on that golden boy who's ready to plop down right in your lap.

Now when you run a relationship with these things in mind, you'll also be tempted to start fights, throw fits, flirt with others, and fail to be there totally on an emotional level. That will definitely keep you from experiencing the kind of contentment that might lead to a satisfactory and long-lasting love life. Always waiting for something better to come along and never appreciating what you have in the moment will most certainly help your relationship blow up like a torpedo hitting a rusty old freighter.

40

♡ ♡ ♡ ♡

Act Morally Superior to Your Lover

Make sure he knows that you're above him in the eyes of the Lord. If he eats meat, become a vegetarian. If he hunts, then avert your eyes from what he brings home and sob.

And for you men, if she applies eye makeup, make sure you let her know that it was tested on innocent rabbits. If she's watching a soap opera, make sure she's aware that the sponsor's commercials feature detergents that have been tested on little kitties.

At all times, let your lover know that you're on the straight runway to heaven, while he's going straight to hell. People like to be told they're morally inferior, and you'll get an immediate bang for your buck by letting your lover know that you're above him in terms of the rules and strictures of your faith—or of human-itarianism, generally. Keep him feeling low, and he'll really thank you for it.

41

♡♡♡♡

Make Up Strict Rules of Conduct to Keep Your Lover Under Total Stalinist Control

Make up rules about what he's allowed to eat—supposedly, of course, for his own good. Don't let him eat the foods he really likes. They'll kill him! Only your homeopathic brew will save him, no matter how tasteless it is.

And don't let him spend much time watching his favorite sports on TV. They're a waste of time in your eyes, and therefore punishable by time in the no-affection gulag if he violates your dictum.

As for her, berate her for reading her favorite trashy novels, and make her feel guilty about it if she does. And be sure she doesn't spend time chatting with her friends on the phone (even though it's so much fun), because it violates rules about spending time constructively.

The great Roman known as Cato the Censor had a rule that slaves on his estate were only allowed to work, eat, or sleep, and nothing else. This is the way it should be with your lover. Keep him regimented and under your control. I mentioned this before in terms of regulating his social life, but be especially strict about everything I've mentioned here . . . and you'll be sure to see dramatic results.

42

♡♡♡♡

Avoid Developing Any Common Interests

Just do your own thing and scoff at your lover's interests. Don't make any effort whatsoever to spend time with her as she does the things she loves.

Don't stay up late watching her favorite old movies with her. Don't walk the dog with her at night. (In, fact, don't even *have* pets, which might constitute a shared interest.) Don't have stimulating conversations around the dinner table where you discuss world events, people you know, or your respective families. What's the point?

Just go your own way, and make sure she knows that you don't give a damn what she cares about or the things she wants you to do with her. You have your own life, after all, and shared interests are for weaklings. You're a mighty and powerful being who has the right to do your own funkadelic thing anytime you want, any way you want.

Common interests? Ixnay.

43

♡♡♡♡

Don't Value Your Lover's Achievements

So what if he just got a raise? Lots of people get raises. So what if he just won a prize in his art class? His work will never be in a museum. Don't let your lover's pitiful little triumphs go to his head. Just keep at him to do better—or else, even better, just ignore him and let his pride wither on the vine. Yes, if you do something modest and decent, *you* expect lavish praise, of course. But when your lover does something estimable, just freaking ignore it now and forever.

People don't need praise and recognition. Or if they do, what business is that of yours? You need only worry about your own praise, not anyone else's. Keep that straight and it will do you a lot of good.

And who cares if it doesn't do anyone else any good? Who counts in this world? You, and that's it.

44

♡♡♡♡

When Things Are Going Really Well, Start a Fight

Think about it for a moment. When things are going really well, isn't that exactly the time when things are a bit . . . um . . . boo-rring? I mean, where's the excitement in just sitting contemplatively with your lover or lying with your bodies intertwined in silence? Where's the joy in that? You want to know the answer? There isn't any!

I'll say it again: Happiness and peace and quiet are boring. No, what you need is excitement and anger and violence and drama. So, start that fight right now. You can always find a reason. The bathroom's a mess. The toothpaste tube isn't straightened out. The toilet seat was left up. Your black sock got lost in the dryer.

There are plenty of reasons to fight if you really look for them. I mean, make up a reason if you need to.

That's it. Get the blood boiling and the juices flowing. Fight, fight, fight. That's the ticket. Now you're talking: Fight, argue, spar, scream, yell, rant, rave—no one can say you have a tired love life now. And brag to all your friends about how much fun it is to make up after a good bout with your lover.

That's right. You know that the best thing you can do for your relationship is to stir things up.

I won't bother to argue this point anymore.

I think you get it.

That's it. Those are the rules.
Now go ahead, you knucklehead.
Go out there and ruin your
love life . . . or save it.

♡♡♡♡

AFTERWORD

♡♡♡♡

I know what you're thinking, you devil. You're saying to yourself, "Hey, don't tell a soul, but I make a lot of those mistakes in my own life. I sure hope no one notices." Well, unfortunately, not only can you be totally sure that someone notices, you can be sure that *everyone* notices.

Most of all, the people you're in love with will take note of your behavior—that is, if you have the *capacity* for love. If you don't, then nothing I've written here can help you.

As you read this book, perhaps you'll say, "Hey, I guess I really do sometimes ask my lover to work for me without expressing gratitude for it." Or maybe you'll acknowledge, "Gee, I suppose I do play phone games and throw tantrums," and "Ha! Maybe I do make fun of my lover's family in front of other people." Or perhaps late at night while you're watching TV in the den you'll suddenly acknowledge, "Well, I guess I really do act as if making love to my mate is a chore."

In fact, unless you're a perfect human being (and who is), you're almost sure to recognize some (or many) of the ruinous characteristics that are laid out in this book.

The simple idea here is: "STOP DOING IT, YOU FOOL!" When you find yourself starting fights over nothing, when you notice that you're always sulking and not telling your lover why, when you realize you're trying to control your lover's life, when you realize you never say "I love you" . . . start behaving in a new and better way. People *can* change. Maybe others can't make them change, but they can change. And if you don't want to be sad and lonely for the rest of your life, you *must* change. (By the way, make sure the change is well under way before you get married, and that it's appreciated. . . .)

People rarely do, in fact, *totally* change, but if they're given an absolutely clear road map, they can modify their behavior somewhat, and if you want to know how to start, here's a clue: Get up off the wrong track, start to make changes right now, and do the very best you can. This advice was given to me long ago by the great editor, Jim Bellows, and it's advice worth heeding: *Start right now, and do the best you can.* Love is a job—albeit a wonderful job—and you have to apply yourself to make it work. But if you *do* work at it, the pay is fabulous.

ABOUT THE AUTHOR

Ben Stein is a lawyer, economist, writer, actor, *Star Search* celebrity judge, and game-show host in Los Angeles, where he lives with his wife, Alexandra; his son, Thomas; and many dogs and cats. He is very active in fund-raising for animal rights and children's rights charities in Los Angeles and throughout the country. Website: **www.benstein.com**

We hope you enjoyed this Hay House book. If you would like
to receive a free catalog featuring additional Hay House books
and products, or if you would like information about the
Hay Foundation, please contact:

Hay House, Inc.
P.O. Box 5100
Carlsbad, CA 92018-5100

(760) 431-7695 or **(800) 654-5126**
(760) 431-6948 (fax) or **(800) 650-5115 (fax)**
www.hayhouse.com

Published and distributed in Australia by:
Hay House Australia, Ltd. • 18/36 Ralph St. • Alexandria NSW 2015
• *Phone:* 612-9669-4299 • *Fax:* 612-9669-4144 •
www.hayhouse.com.au

Published and distributed in the United Kingdom by:
Hay House UK, Ltd. • Unit 202, Canalot Studios •
222 Kensal Rd., London W10 5BN • *Phone:* 44-20-8962-1230 •
Fax: 44-20-8962-1239 • www.hayhouse.co.uk

Published and distributed in the Republic of South Africa by:
Hay House SA (Pty), Ltd., P.O. Box 990, Witkoppen 2068 •
Phone/Fax: 2711-7012233 • orders@psdprom.co.za

Distributed in Canada by:
Raincoast • 9050 Shaughnessy St., Vancouver, B.C. V6P 6E5 •
Phone: (604) 323-7100 • *Fax:* (604) 323-2600

Sign up via the Hay House USA Website to receive the Hay House
online newsletter and stay informed about what's going on with
your favorite authors. You'll receive bimonthly announcements
about: Discounts and Offers, Special Events, Product Highlights,
Free Excerpts, Giveaways, and more!